Can God Trust *Yo*

Can God Trust ***You*** with Trouble?

Reverend Stanley Moore

Can God Trust *You* with Trouble?

Rev. Stanley Moore

Pastor, Progressive Baptist Church

with

Colonel Burl Randolph, Jr., Retired, U.S. Army

Rev. Stanley Moore

Can God Trust *You* with Trouble?

ISBN-10: 1516922905
ISBN-13: 978-1516922901

My appreciation to Reverend Teresa Ambler, who provided the "spiritual editorial eyes" to this work.

Cover photo: Man in a black suit with a black umbrella by solarseven.

Cover graphics: Burl Randolph, Jr., MyWingman, LLC.

Portions of *When You Lose Someone You Love* by Randy Peterson used by permission of Lincoln, IL: Publications International, Ltd.

BISAC: Religion/Faith

Dedication

***This book is dedicated to my parents*:**

Deacon Clyde and Mrs. Pearlie Mae Moore

This book is dedicated to my parents, Deacon Clyde Moore and Mrs. Pearlie Mae Moore. Both have gone on to their eternal rewards, duly earned and well deserved. My father, Deacon Clyde, knew my calling to the ministry before I did, and I attempt to emulate daily, his steadfastness in serving the Lord. My mother, Mrs. Pearlie Mae, is the reason I am who I am. Picking up where my father left off, mom asked me, "What took so long for you to answer God's call?" I have answered God's call daily for the last 25 years, because of the love both provided me.

Reverend Stanley Moore

Acknowledgements

I want to knowledge first and foremost:
My wife **Connie**.

You pay a dear price for sharing your husband with so many. I want you to know how much I appreciate, and love you for who you are, and all that you do. Thank you for your love, support, understanding, and sacrifice.

To my children Kelton, Suzanna, Mel, and Evin:
For being prayerful, thoughtful, and understanding throughout the entire process.

To my sister "Earlene" and my brother "Arthur":
For your prayers, words of encouragement, and the bond we share.

To my brother in Christ, Colonel Burl Randolph, Jr., Retired, US Army. Thank you for surrendering your gifts and talents for the kingdom. Thank you for walking with me and assisting me with this project. You are the greatest.

And to my Progressive Church Family:
You all have been with me through all the changes, and trials of ministry. Thank you for standing with me through the valley moments and rejoicing with me in the times of peace. Love you all.

Most of all, I thank God, for in Him I live, I move, and I have my being.

Contents

Preface

We are all familiar with the stewardship of being trusted with treasure. We understand the value and security concerns with treasure. There are professional experts who manage and invest in treasure. When kinfolks are aware of your treasure, they see you as the family banker. When enemies are aware of your treasure, they look for ways to steal the treasure. Therefore, people with treasure strive to keep it a secret. Pastor Stanley Moore has raised a serious stewardship question:

"Can God trust you with trouble?"

This is an unfamiliar stewardship assignment. We understand immediately the value and need of security with treasure, but when you are steward of troubles, the value is difficult to see. Troubles are public and whispered from one to another. There are no professional experts who can help when it comes to troubles. Like Job's three friends, they counseled best when they kept silent (Job 13:5).

I observed Pastor Moore walk out his stewardship assignment. What he taught me will last a lifetime. I thought troubles had no value, but I gazed in the wrong direction. The value is above, not below. The treasure is above because God is real, heaven is real, and the power of heaven is real.

God has trusted Pastor Stanley Moore with troubles. He walked in the midst of Progressive Baptist Church congregation, his family, and our community and he preached without ever saying a word about his troubles. Although I knew his troubles, I did not understand how to reply to his stewardship question:

"Can God trust you with trouble?

Pastor Moore answered the question in this book. God is up to something when He trusts you with troubles:

To be trusted with troubles gives access to the treasure of heaven.

When God trust one with troubles, all the power of heaven sustains, and the supply of heaven flows without limit, delay, or excuse.

I thank God that Pastor Moore has shared his journey in these pages. When you read his testimony, you will understand why he is still here. I will look at troubles differently from this day forward.

Reverend P. Wonder Harris
Pastor, Mt. Zion Missionary Baptist Church
East Moline, Illinois

Forward

I give honor to God and to my spiritual leader, Pastor Stanley Moore. Although Pastor Moore often tells the congregation that he has never served in the military, his resolve to fulfill his assignment would rival the tenacity of Former Secretary of State and Chairman of the Joint Chiefs of Staff, retired Army General Colin Powell. Pastor Moore's passion to continue the task of leading the congregation while embroiled in a personal battle, forced me to ask myself the question:

Can God trust <u>me</u> with trouble?

This question may be as ancient as time, but also as contemporary and progressive as the man required to answer it: Pastor Stanley Moore. God spoke directly to Pastor Moore four years ago at the advent of an unbelievable odyssey of events initiated by the murder of his beloved youngest daughter, TeNille 'Neal' Moore.

On an abnormal Sunday morning with a packed and waiting congregation, God asked Pastor Moore:

"Can I Trust You with Trouble?"

and Pastor Moore answered, "*Yes Lord*". Unknowingly, Pastor Moore would be tried and tested not once, but three additional times within the next 12 months. Challenged to endure the deaths of Darlene and Brenda, two of his three sisters, and his mother, Mrs. Pearlie Mae

Moore, Pastor Moore began to ask *himself* if God could trust him with trouble.

I have only known Pastor Moore for a brief period; however, the epiphany that occurred to me some six months after assisting with this book is that Pastor Moore's story is the vehicle that God is using to ask all of us:

"Can God Trust *You* with Trouble?"

I realized that *You* must be capitalized, italicized, and underlined for the question to become *personal* to the reader. Pastor Moore chose to some degree, to share his journey of faith and grief with us, not just as a Pastor - but as daddy, father, husband, brother, son, friend, and faithful servant. Pastor Moore's journey of faith is a desperate deliverance of one man learning how to be a better believer and not a bitter servant in a plight that all grievers must face when walking in the valley of death. God also chose for Pastor Moore to share his voyage of faith to increase our faith in Him as the Almighty God.

With happiness securely incarcerated by grief, God showed Pastor Moore how hope unlocks happiness. Consequently, God also wanted Pastor Moore to identify and deal with the most malignant oddity of our time: ***It***. ***It*** may be in the form of emotional hurt, continuous pain, or physical distress but if left unattended, ***It*** can kill you. A fervent man of God, Pastor Moore's story is one of communing with God during his darkest hours, not as a Pastor, but as Stanley Moore. Leaders are not always afforded the luxury of expressing feelings, depending on friends, or the comforting support of family, but must fall back on the only thing that can sustain them – Faith, the kind of faith that believes and trust in God. Faith in feelings, friends, and family is fine, but none of them can save you from ***It,*** because only God can do that.

As I listened to his sermons every week, Pastor Moore has shown his compassionate and eminent faith by sharing his deeply personal story with the world. So, when the question is asked:

"Can God Trust <u>You</u> with Trouble?"

we can all have the same answer: *Yes Lord.* I hope you find Pastor Moore's story as informative, enlightening, uplifting, and spiritual as I have. God Bless you, God Speed, and good reading.

Burl W. Randolph, Jr.
Colonel, US Army, Retired
President, MyWingman, LLC
Davenport, IA

It is with great sadness that I convey to the readers that in March 2022, Reverend Stanley Moore went to his great reward while in the service of the Lord. Pastor Moore, as he referred to be called, took care of his wife, Mrs. Connie Moore, who died in March 2021, while pastoring his congregation. Until the very end, he was the epitome of leadership, giving his all for those he loved, and those he never knew. In honor to his memory, I hope that you will read, apply, and review Pastor Moore's work so that you will know for yourself if *God can trust you with trouble*. Dr. Burl Randolph, Jr., DM, Coauthor

Introduction

Being a man or woman of faith does not shield one from the tests of life, nor does it suspend the feelings or emotions those tests may bring. I believe there is a season for all things. Even though it has taken me three years to sit down, process, accept, and reflect on the tragedies and losses I experienced – now is that season. The bible states in Ecclesiastes chapter three; verse one that "To everything there is a season, and a time to every purpose under the heaven." Now is the time and purpose for this book.

I never intended to default or delay in the writing of this book. Let us remember, I Corinthians chapter 14; verses 33 and 40 indicates that,

"For God is not the author of confusion, but of peace, as in all the churches of the saints. Let all things be done decently and in order."

Undoubtedly, many others may have experienced tragedies of the same magnitude, but as a Pastor, God uses me in a different manner. I am called to teach others about His grace and mercy, to never give up hope, and to keep the faith. Though other people have encouraged me to share this story much sooner, the time, season, and purpose - all needed to be in alignment. The retelling of the events that formed this story could not cause confusion, but bring peace and encouragement to the readers. The decency in this is that although God works in our faith, He does so to provide comfort and support in our time of need.

As promised in Joshua chapter one; verse nine, *"Be strong and of good courage: be not afraid, neither be thou dismayed: For the Lord thy God is with thee whithersoever thou goest."*

The bible is replete with words of comfort for those who study and believe it, such as Proverbs chapter three; verses five and six, "Trust in the Lord with all of thy heart and lean not on thy own understanding. In all thy ways acknowledge Him, and He shall direct thy paths."

My hope is that this book can help guide you through life's trials and tests to achieve God's triumphs for your life and the lives of those you impact daily, as you trust Him.

Reverend Stanley Moore
Pastor, Progressive Baptist Church
Davenport, IA

Part I
Finding Faith, Again

Of all God's precepts, I believe faith may be my favorite. Please, do not read what I did not write, or hear what I am not saying: I love all of God's precepts. Of the big three: Faith, Hope, and Love however, I believe faith often gets a raw deal. Love is the most often sang, sought, and sulked about. Hope is the second one most often heard, heralded, and hurt about. But faith, who croons, craves, or cries about it?

Now faith is the substance of things hoped for, the evidence of things not seen (Hebrews chapter 11, verse 1).

During my odyssey of discovering if God could trust me with trouble, family, friends, and even foes often asked me: How did you keep your faith? The answer is rather simple: I kept my faith in God because God kept His faith in me!

I entitled Part I of this book: Finding Faith, Again, because through the grieving process, love is shown by others, and hope is what we rest on, but faith is what's tested. What I call The Foundations of Faith, are that: Godly faith is unstoppable, endures, and produces the Three C's of Faith: Confidence, Conviction, and Calm. Faith develops our confidence in life, which leads to the conviction that all storms are temporary and creates the calm one can possess in the middle of a storm. Although God kept me through it all, my faith in Him, His principles, and His promises is what allowed me to keep the faith. Staying close to God is what will allow you to Find Faith, Again, should yours become shaken during the grieving process.

Chapter One

Faith, Not Feelings

Weapons of Mass Destruction (WMD) is often how we view the trials of life. While it may *feel* as if life's trials are destroying our will, desires, or sense of purpose, it is really all part of the process I call Weapons of Mass Instruction -WMI, not WMD. God's WMI is a tool to make us better not bitter, so do not despair, lose hope, or give in to life's pressures. This means God allows the less pleasant and sometimes the most devastating life experiences and challenges to occur as vehicles for instruction. God desires to prepare us for what He has predestined for our lives here on earth, so we must remember: Trials are winnable, and tests are passable, because God will always provide the necessary WMI to ensure a victory through Jesus Christ; who is the author and finisher of our faith. Even when we encounter the abnormal, God has our best interest at heart.

The Trial: *An Abnormal Sunday*

It was an abnormal Sunday. The events of that Sunday would change my life forever. On July 24, 2011, a beautiful Sunday morning unfolded while I sat in my office as I often did and still do, meditating and preparing to deliver the morning message. It was an abnormal Sunday because of the uncharacteristic atmosphere in the church. There were as many if not more people in the church that morning, than on an Easter Sunday. Little did I know that chairs would line the aisles, parishioners would crowd the vestibule, and the choir would remain in the choir stand behind the pulpit because the pews were full, exceeding the 200-limit capacity. Though this all sounds good, to have such a waiting crowd at the end of July created an *Abnormal Sunday*.

Even though my phone rings often on Sunday mornings, I usually do not answer it. I am usually in a concentration mode, not wanting to interrupt my worship preparation. On this morning however, I noticed the phone number as being that of my baby girl, Latarsha. I knew it must have been important because she knew her Dad's longstanding Sunday morning routine. I never would have expected answering that phone would change my life forever and begin a trail of events beyond my vast imagination.

When I answered, I heard Latarsha's distressed and troubled voice calling for her dad:

"***Daddy, daddy, daddy***," she shouted.

Then, I heard several gun shots followed by silence. I will never forget that moment, as I now know that the shots had silenced my baby forever. In a daze and a haze, the events that occurred next are only recalled in reflections, and the actions executed from muscle memory. I recall hanging up the phone and one of the ministers sitting across from me, Minister Anthony Griffin asking me, "*Pastor, are you ok?*" I could hear the voice, but the noise of what I had just heard over the phone outweighed my abilities to respond. Minister Griffin asked again, "*Pastor, are you alright?*" but I remained paralyzed by the events I believed in my mind had just occurred and were later confirmed. The next voice I heard provided me the <u>first key lesson</u> in my trials of tests and trust:

"Learn to listen *for* the voice and not *to* the noise."

A Moment of Reflection

About 'Neal'

LaTarsha TeNille Moore

I chose at this point to tell you a little about *Daddy's Baby Girl*, which is the best way to describe my beloved 'Neal'. We called LaTarsha TeNille Moore 'Neal' because both LaTarsha and TeNille might be considered rather formal around the house. The youngest child and a girl amongst a bunch of rambunctious boys between her and her older sister, Neal always knew how to calm a situation and keep her brothers in line. In her adult life, Neal did not depart far from her childhood spirit of keeping folks in line. Neal served 11 years as a security guard with St. Jude Children's Research Hospital in East Memphis, Tennessee. She also worked an additional job to make sure all ends could meet. Neal loved the Lord with all her heart and showed it as a wife, mother, daughter, sister, and friend with all her heart. She lived well regarded, well respected, and well spoken. A word from Neal always seemed to put people at ease.

Although my daughter, Neal became a trusted friend, advisor, and my spiritual partner in the Lord - which is what gives me such solace. Neal left us sooner than we were ready, taken from us only one day after her 32nd birthday. Though I may feel that way, God allows what He allows, and I know that Neal resides in the arms of our Lord and Savior Jesus Christ.

Serving the Lord all her life, Neal knew what it meant to be a Christian. Neal also blessed us with a grandson, Justyn, who keeps her perfect memory alive. What I recall most about that morning is I received calls from two of the most beloved and cherished in my life:

First Neal, and then God. I can only surmise that both calls were in preparation for things to come. As a leader, faith is required to function during life's most dire circumstances. I had a waiting congregation that required a word from God, not Stanley Moore because after all, I would soon tell God that He could trust me with trouble.

The Test: *A Waiting Congregation*

In essence, faith is all about trust. At that point, I did not know who or what to trust, because my senses were on overload. *Who* to trust became abundantly clear when I heard a voice ask:

"Can I trust you with trouble?"

Although bewildered by the events, I knew the voice came from God. We all operate on what the scholars call mental models - the way we view and process things in life. My mental model had encountered a major mental block that obscured my focus, but God immediately arrested my attention by assuring me that He would never leave me nor forsake. I chose the phrase *arrested my attention* because in my mental state at the time, God had to capture and detain my mind.

A Numbed Spirit

I have endured many medical maladies throughout my life, but none paralyzed me. As the deacons called for the processional of the clergy, a complete and total numbness engulfed my body to the point of being mute for the vast majority of the service. I recall some sights and sounds but could not utter a word to truly participate in worship. As we

proceeded down the center aisle so familiar to me over the previous six years, seeing the unusual abundance of people in the church seemed *abnormal*. My wife Connie (unknowing of the phone call), sat in her customary seat on the front row left pew facing the pulpit. The choir sang with majesty, passion, and reverence unlike any other time, the church was filled beyond capacity, and the Spirit reigned high. All these elements created an *Abnormal Sunday* morning at the end of July 2011.

As I sat in my usual seat, I could hear, see, clap, and I may have even smiled a bit, but sat in absolute numbness, unable to utter a word. I felt as if my heart had been ripped from me, but I could not confirm the events that I believed I had heard over the phone. I remained numb, mute in both voice and spirit until the time arrived to present the sermon. Any doubt I ever had completely vanished for I knew that God's Holy Spirit had complete control over me.

An Arrested Attention

God took hold of me and directed that I look at the waiting congregation, postured to hear a word from Him through me. God asked me again:

"Can I trust you with trouble?"

This time I could answer the question and stated "*Yes Lord, Here I Am*." I may have only answered *Yes* to God's question, but that brought <u>the second lesson</u> in my trials of test and trust:

> Whenever we say *Yes* to God, we are in effect saying *Here I Am*, which means *Lord, use me as You see fit*.

At the time, I had an unfit *feeling*, but God gave me hope and peace that surpassed all understanding, which made me fit for my assignment. Pastor Charles "Chuck" R. Swindoll once wrote that "We all need hope! When we are enduring life's most difficult times, we need to believe that a positive outcome is possible. Only in hope can we wait for that positive outcome." Swindoll (2012) further wrote that:

> *When we are trapped in a tunnel of misery, Hope points to the light at the end of the tunnel. When we are discouraged, Hope lifts our spirits. When we are tempted to quit, Hope keeps us going. When we lose our way and confusion blurs the destination, Hope dulls the edge of panic. When we must endure the consequences of God's decisions, Hope fuels our recovery.*

I had the same hope at that moment, which any parent would have for their child: That the situation remained well, and what I thought I had heard would not come to pass.

For the first time in 21 years of ministry, I knew that the answers to the test God administered to me were provided directly from Him. The events that occurred on that day are but a blur to my natural mind.

I recall seeing a packed church as the processional occurred as usual. In my mind's eye I saw my wife Connie, but at the same time could not see her. The choir sang, deacons prayed, I preached a sermon, and 14 people were saved that day, joining the ranks of the Christian body. Those events however were all completely and totally God-led and inspired, because I have no true recollection of them from the physical perspective. It was and remains an *Abnormal Sunday*.

God wanted to know if He could trust me with trouble as He had always trusted me when none existed: Because He wanted me to know just how valuable I am beyond Stanley Moore. Neal choosing to call me in her final moments provided me the sign that she trusted me with trouble, and now God wanted to know if He could do the same. Although I passed the first iteration, little did I know the test had multiple parts, given at different times, covering different subjects but all related to one theme that the Lord wanted me to become versed in: Grief. Without any further instruction, the testing is how my trust developed for dealing with telling the tragedy.

The Trust: *Telling the Tragedy*

I recall Former Army Chief of Staff General Gordon R. Sullivan penned a national bestselling book entitled *Hope is Not a Method.* Biblically, that pronouncement may be questionable because as Hebrews chapter 11, verse one indicates "Now faith is the substance of things hoped for, the evidence of things not seen". Because certainty of death is the only 100 percent in life, every plan, process, or prediction has an element of hope for success. The <u>third lesson</u> in my trial of test and trust:

Although hope may not be a method, manner, or mode, hope is a motivator that provides the means to keep our minds moving in a positive direction.

Faith and hope occur through continuous trust in God's word to never leave nor forsake us.

After departing the pulpit, I suspended greeting parishioners and moved directly into my office and sat in my chair. That aberrant behavior on my part added to the atmosphere of an *Abnormal Sunday.* Shortly thereafter my sons Scooter (Kelton) and Evin arrived.

Scooter said "*Dad, it's bad*".

I asked, "*How bad*?" and he said:

"***TeNille is dead***".

Evin arrived right behind Scooter and said, "*He killed her*".

He was Neal's husband. My worst fears confirmed, I remained calm because that is who I am as a person, what God placed in my spirit as the pastor, and the requirement for a leader: To remain calm to instill calm in others. God pressed pause on my emotional pain in the pulpit, and allowed me to complete my assignment, and continued to do so after confirmation of my worst fears.

Church members were inquiring about the abrupt changes in my processes and posture and attempted to visit me in the office. One of the deaconesses, Deaconess Jewel Taylor, came into my office, embraced me, and reminded me that I had plenty of prayer partners. She also told me one of the most profound aspects in processing this event:

"You need to be daddy now and take care of the rest of your family."

As I went home and attempted to process the events of the day, I had to come to terms with the events to gain new knowledge. Even though I know knowledge is defined as justified true belief (Feldman, 2003), there were no means for me to justify what had happened to my baby girl, and although the events may have been true, they remained unbelievable. Although friends and family were plentiful, faith is what I had to carry me through.

Why Faith Not Feelings: *A Leaders Requirement*

As the evening progressed and the phone rang non-stop, a fellow pastor, Pastor P.W. Harris, arrived at our home and we began to pray. At that time, I had not even cried because the most difficult tasks lay ahead. I discovered that effective leadership required faith not feelings because there are always so many people that depend on the leader for strength, and I just happened to be that leader. Being the spouse of a leader can sometimes be just as arduous, and my wife Connie has always been my rock. She remained resolute in supporting me every step of the way, and I cannot thank her enough through it all. God continued to carry me through as my sons drove me to Tennessee to identify Neal and begin making the funeral arrangements. Arriving on the scene, faith once again averted a near tragic situation.

Faith Not Fighting

The scene that greeted us when we arrived at Neal's residence is reminiscent of what we have seen on television when a young African American male is shot and killed: Supreme anger. Angry family members from both sides were postured to wage war in the streets of East Memphis, Tennessee over this tragic event. Unknown to me at the time how brutally Neal had been murdered, I knew that she would never sanction any amount of violence on her behalf.

As I exited the truck, I beseeched the crowd not to engage in any sort of fighting or violence, but to disperse and allow cooler heads to prevail. I am not a military man; however, I do serve in the Army of the Lord. Faith not feelings is what allowed me to maintain the courage to face and calm down angry people who I later discovered had an arsenal of various weapons. Little did I know or could have imagined how much faith I would need for the events ahead.

Faith Not Violence

Whenever an event this tragic and brutal occurs, raw feelings are exposed that could lead to violence. As we returned to Neal's house that Monday evening with a candlelight vigil in progress, 16 or more police cars were present and a helicopter flew overhead. The situation had poised the crowd for violence, which answered why God had been continually asking me:

"Stanley, Can I Trust You with Trouble?"

Answering *Yes Lord* continually, God gave me the strength, courage, and faith to dispel the feelings in that crowd by exclaiming:

"*There will be no more killing. She's gone, he's gone, and violence will not serve a purpose.*"

My advice extended to my sons as well, who were rightfully distraught over the senseless murder of their baby sister and wanted a means to express that anger. God continued to keep the pause on my pain to allow me to continue the assignment and avert the violence, but I needed extended faith as well. In our weakened state is when the devil is at his best because it requires less of his limited power. Faith continued to play a significant role in helping me to process the events while avoiding the tricks of the devil.

Faith Not Fear

People often say that a lack of faith is what causes fear. As human beings, there is no one element that might cause us to be fearful. Many of the greatest victories in the bible were accomplished through people who exhibited fear. Fear gripped Mary when the angel Michael came upon her. Joseph struggled through fear when he saw the angel, Gabriel. The disciples were constantly fearful, even in Jesus' presence. In each example, lack of faith did not cause fear, but a lack of knowledge. A simple phrase for a lack of knowledge is The Unknown.

As I returned to the hotel, the totality of the situation began to formulate in my mind. As I began to process the events, another event occurred that revealed The Unknown: I spoke with Neal. That event could have caused fear to set in but instead, the Lord allowed it me to speak with Neal as plainly and clearly as I speak to people every day. The Lord allowed me to ask Neal:

"*Baby, are you okay*?"

Neal answered me just as plain as day and said:

"Dad, you taught me what to do. I'm okay - my question is, are you ok?"

That Unknown: The true status of my daughter, allowed me to begin grasping the reality of the situation. I heard Neal's voice so clearly at that time it was unimaginable, but I have never heard her voice again since that day. Even in hearing her voice, fear could have gripped me, but faith did not allow it, and my assignment continued.

Brothers and sisters, when we say our final farewell to loved ones, hope of life beyond the grave gets us through our grief. Believe me; hope is not optional but essential to our survival, and truly becomes a method. The logic in hope does not reside in our feelings but by our faith, which is where God works with us.

When life hurts and dreams begin to fade, nothing helps like hope, and faith not feelings is what carries us through.

Faith not feelings and hope not heartache must carry us through, because the enemy will continue to attack us in our valley moments, and Pastors are not exempt!

Chapter Two
A Focused Faith

The loss of a child may be as devastating as it gets for a parent. The devil, however, will always attack you in your wilderness or valley moments. When Jesus entered the wilderness after 40 days of fasting, the devil attacked him at the most vulnerable point: In the valley moment when he had the greatest needs and seemed at his weakest (Matthew 4:1). *Seemed at his weakest* is the testament to focusing your faith, because things are not always as they seem. God will again ask the question, *Can I Trust You with Trouble,* because trouble continued to follow me in ways I never imagined.

A Reason to Focus on Faith

I often tell my congregation that thanksgiving can be found in six simple words:

"He woke me up this morning!"

Much the same may be said about faith. The next tasks I believed were the hardest in my life and may still be: The requirements to identify Neal's body. Coupled with making all of the funeral arrangements is something no parent would ever imagine or should ever have to endure. As written earlier, I did not know the brutality of her murder, and still do not understand it. I needed to super-size the focus on my faith at that point, to give Neal the respect her life deserved, regardless of the circumstances.

Faith is a powerful weapon in the arsenal of God's Army, and I am thankful every day for God's tender mercies. The requirement to identify Neal's body could have, should have, and would have sent me over the edge, if not for God's loving hand. As I began to make the arrangements for Neal, I needed to also consider the raw pain and emotions of Kelton (also known as Scooter) and Evin. God gave me the strength to continue focusing on my faith in Him as my Father, so that my sons could focus their faith on me as their father. Now, I make no claims to be a deity or on par with God, but as we are all formed in the spiritual image of God, my sons needed to see Him in me at that time to provide a degree of calmness for their lives and a development of their faith in God.

As I went about making Neal's funeral arrangements, my baby sister Darlene arrived and helped me every step of the way. As we rode in Darlene's car, finalizing the arrangements for the service and picking out the casket, Darlene uttered the most curious comment:

"*I want this exact casket for my funeral too*".

Undoubtedly, I did not know that wish would come to fruition within the next few months. I needed to continue focusing my faith on the situation at hand and continued to discover just how much each event would test of my faith.

Tests Reveals Faith

Testing awakens our dormant faith to become active, so faith will manifest itself by the test it encounters. Faith is only proven during trouble not triumphs. We will never know how much faith we have or how strong it is, until it is tested. Our faith is only as strong as the test it survives, so, what is the key to overcoming the storm? We overcome the storm by focusing on the faith, not the test. Another key to passing the faith test is to identify the tester: God or ourselves?

As I continued to plan for Neal's funeral, I also arranged to preside over the service and eulogy. At that point my cousin, Bishop Connie L. Moore (this Connie is a male), mentioned to me that I had no requirement to be Pastor Moore on that day, but needed to be Daddy Moore. I did not need to preside over the service, but over my family. When I removed myself from that part of the equation, it provided me more time to reflect on the events, and my faith. This allowed my cousin, Bishop Moore, to eulogize Neal in a manner only a family member could.

Love is a verb because it always denotes action, and my Progressive Baptist Church family epitomized their love for me and my family in our greatest time of need. The funeral for Neal occurred in Arkansas and the logistics of the event are minor however, the arrival of six carloads of parishioners from Davenport, Iowa, over 600 miles away, provided a major uplifting to my spirit. All the moving parts of an event and tragedy of this magnitude is why God requires a focused faith to trust us with trouble, and to help illuminate tests.

Test Explained

Godly faith guarantees that there is life beyond the test however, how do we shift our attention from the test? Shifting our focus to our faith enables us to move past the test and continue living in the manner God intended. Focusing on the faith and not the test or storms of life is vitally important for God to be able to trust us with trouble for three reasons (James 1:2-4).

First, only looking at test or storms creates an imbalance within our lives. Only focusing on one thing in life: death, creates an imbalance with second and third order effects. Second, the imbalance tends to grow, possibly larger than the reality of the situation, if we gaze at it too long. Third and most important, if we allow the imbalance to grow, we begin to value our feelings over our faith and that obscures the facts. Once the facts are obscured, so are the truths. So then, how *Can God Trust You with Trouble?* when the truths or facts of the situation cannot be seen? Focusing on faith not feelings is how we move past the tests and storms in our lives.

To say that Neal's death did not test my faith would be a colossal lie. Many people brag about faith but only because that faith has never been tested. God *allows* testing in our lives to reveal the depth and quality of our faith. In our valley moments, faith is the best and possibly only means to fight temptation.

Faith Can Foil Temptations

While enduring trials, many succumb to temptations by confusing them with test. God will not allow us to be tested beyond our ability to overcome (I Corinthians 10:13). That means God controls the measure of our test, but who controls the measure of our response? Each of us controls the measure of our response, however, without focused faith; our response may give way to temptations. Temptations are natural, normal, and based on our earthly desires. Thus, what is good *to* you is not always good *for* you.

After arriving back home in Davenport, Iowa, delving deeper into ministry to avoid the grieving process is the temptation that became good *to* me however, not good *for* me. There is a reason and a season for grieving that we must all pass through, and attempting to bottle up or circumvent the process may have dire consequences. We know grief brings with it a chorus of feelings and behaviors: Denial, anger, disbelief, loneliness, fear, worry, impatience, shock, regret, and uncertainty.

Because grief is such a powerful but necessary process, a focused faith is crucial to reaching the chasm of freedom that brings remembrance, growth, and hope. As James espoused in chapter one, verses 12-17:

"But each one is tempted when, by his own desire, he is dragged away and enticed."

Grief therefore requires a coping mechanism beyond the realm of this world - a focused faith. Although I believed I had a focused faith, little did I know this test of faith had multiple parts. Based on this experience, I would highly recommend a student should always receive confirmation of a passing grade on a test prior to proclaiming victory.

Why God Requires a Focused Faith

We must understand that the trials we endure are common tests that come our way as part of life. God allows those common tests for the proving and maturing of our faith. Although at the time it may not seem like it, how we deal with death is a common test. Each and every one must experience it and no one can escape it. A focused faith grants us the ability to discern the sources of test in our lives and is critical to our ability to live successfully beyond the test.

Remaining focused on my faith, I did not fully recognize the need to grieve. My church graciously asked me if I needed a respite of a few months and I fervently told them that God's work could not wait. Little did I realize that I would need that respite. Five short months later, the second part of the test would occur, and I would lose another baby: My baby sister Darlene.

Remembering Darlene

Middle sister Brenda on the left, with the spirited baby sister Darlene in front.

Diagnosed with lymphoma, a disease of the lymph nodes often referred to as Hodgkin's disease, Darlene never let it slow her down. She accepted her condition and lived life to the fullest until the very end. Because my baby sister helped me plan the home going for my baby girl, you can imagine the devastation I encountered when she died. Darlene never complained, moaned, or groaned about her condition, but simply enjoyed the life she had. Though I am not the oldest in the family, God chooses who he chooses to lead us in times of trouble. Having completed the arrangements for Neal just five months earlier, I knew exactly what to do for Darlene, especially since she had already given me guidance on what she desired. A focused faith allows you to remember the seemingly strange occurrences for your future reference.

Although planning a funeral is already difficult, Darlene died on January 8, 2012, just after the 2011 holiday season. This brought even greater despair, and compounded matters: How to tell mama. Pondering with my siblings Earlene, Brenda, and Arthur on how to tell mama about Darlene, proved to be an exercise in futility. When we decided to tell mama, she initiated the conversation by telling us "I know my baby's dead, so why try to hide it?" Again, test come in many forms and God allowed the four of us to pass that test without any effort on our part. Though none of us felt significantly better, the same strength God provided me

for my family, He now provided to my mama for hers. The calmness also permitted Darlene's son, Karrico Moore, some degree of solace in processing his mother's death, and did not create a fractured faith (I Peter 4:7).

A Focused versus a Fractured Faith

A focused faith has granted me the ability and serenity to live beyond my multiple tests, and to fight any temptations or self-induced tests that would tear me down. I wrote this chapter for those early in the grieving process because I did not know the immensity to the question *Can God Trust You with Trouble?* Focused faith is Godly faith that He will eventually but not immediately, see us through the tests.

A focused faith believes in God's power versus His performance. God performs for us daily by providing the air we breathe, aligning the moon and stars, and controlling the atmosphere, all through His incredible power. Godly faith is trusting in God, regardless of when He decides to use His power on our behalf. Godly faith believes amid God's silence.

A fractured faith is the turn that many people take during grief, and when God is silent, not knowing what to believe and only wanting solace from the pain. In the microwave generation, we want instantaneous everything, to include answers from God, and the lack of answers to our pain may fracture our faith. This is why a focused faith is required because a Godly faith makes us better not bitter, to endure the heartaches that common testing brings. Godly faith is a focused faith that accepts that yesterday is history that cannot be changed, tomorrow is a mystery that only God controls, but the present is our gift of today. This may all sound easy and even contrite but do not be deceived: Grief will steal your happiness and rob you of your joy if you allow it, and trouble may continue to come in many forms.

At this point the reader may ask: What happens when one cannot recover from a fractured faith? God is a God of choices, not convenience. The recovery or repair of a fractured faith comes by three means: Prayer, supplication, and time. Praying is our communication with God, and supplication is our fervent prayers to God. God wants to know that we are sincere in our request to Him and are willing to petition and wait for His reply. As trouble may continue to come, and a situation may seem desperate, a constant line of communication with God over time is required to be delivered from a fractured faith.

Notes

....

....

....

....

....

....

....

....

....

....

Chapter Three

A Desperate Deliverance

Though beginning a paragraph with a question may seem improper, we often begin and end each day with questions: God, why is this happening to me? God, what did I do to deserve this? God, when will these trials end? God, how can I make things better? When people are in distress, questions consume their thoughts. When people become desperate, irrational thinking consumes their mind. But only when people seek deliverance, do they seek God.

A desperate deliverance, however, requires Godly measures in distressing times. Although distressing times may be fraught with obstacles, there are always options and when there are options, there are also opportunities. Obstacles, options, and opportunities occurred for the family to survive the next round of tragedies.

A Beckoning for Brenda

Almost 11 months after losing Neal and Darlene, my attempts at normalcy were a daily struggle. Trying to understand the 'why's' of Neal's murder haunted me daily. Though I needed answers to calm my spirit, my mind needed to remain engaged with the Lord's business. I believed and used this as the means to address my grief and sought solace through helping others. As I drove to visit my mother Mrs. Pearlie Mae

Moore, and my sister Earlene Alexander in Davenport, Florida, I stopped through Atlanta to visit my middle sister Brenda.

To my surprise, my brother-in-law George Williams, Brenda's husband, told me of her hospitalization, and her grave condition. Being admitted to the hospital on the previous Friday, Brenda had lapsed into a coma, remained unresponsive during my hospital visit, and the doctors did not expect her to live. George told me that Brenda had only come out of the coma once: On her son Barry's birthday on June 24, 2012, which is the day after my birthday.

As we praised God and believed that a miracle loomed near, Brenda lapsed back into a coma, lived for another week, and died on her daughter Catina's birthday on June 30, 2012. Brenda's other three sons: Marvin, Anthony, and Javen were just as shocked and devastated as the rest of us by the suddenness of losing Brenda. The Lord, however, had already beckoned for Brenda.

Though I had never shared it with the family before, when Neal died, I saw a vision of Brenda's death. Although I did not know how, when, or why, I knew that Brenda would depart sooner than later to meet the Lord. George, Brenda's husband, agreed with me when I told him,

"*We lost Brenda when Darlene left*".

The closeness of my two sisters appeared almost twin-like, and the loss of Darlene broke Brenda's heart probably as much as losing Neal broke mine.

With the loss of a third female family member, what had I learned at that point? Truthfully, I did not have time to reflect on the significance of the events, because when I returned to Memphis, TN, my mother would not let me out of her sight, literally. Mama could not speak much because as we all knew; the end drew near. The end came for mama just two weeks after Brenda passed, and close to the anniversary of Neal's death. Mama's death would provide for me, the answer to the question of what I would need to learn through all the trials and test.

Notes

....

....

....

....

....

....

....

....

....

....

Teacher till the End

Mrs. Pearlie Mae Moore

Mrs. Pearlie Mae Moore with son, Pastor Stanley Moore

The bible contains numerous passages regarding a mother's love. Mothers provide nature, nurture, and primary caregiving in our lives. To be a good mother requires being a good woman, with none better than Pearlie Moore, in my opinion. Through every phase of my life, I learned something from my mama.

I learned the full force of a mother's love after our daddy died. Mama ensured that we continued to move forward in God and would not allow a fractured faith to occur. My mother fully supported my call to the ministry and wondered what took me so long to answer the call. Mama knew before I knew that God's calling would consume the remainder of my life, once I accepted the calling. And now in death, mama provided me her final lesson, which I am certain God ordained.

With mama fading fast, my brother Arthur and I stood right by her side every step of the way. When we entered mama's room on the morning of July 21, 2012, she had gone on to glory, and I gently closed her eyes as Arthur departed the room. A familiar acquaintance returned during that moment of mama's death: ***Numbness***, the same feeling that visited when Neal died. Although I chose devastation as the word to describe how my oldest sister Earlene and older brother Arthur and I were feeling that word seems far too mild. To give you a perspective on how I felt, this passage, which I will explain in full later, truly sums it up:

Losing Neal meant losing a piece of what I gave her, but losing mama meant losing a piece of what she gave me.

With Neal murdered 11 months prior, Darlene passing just five months later, Brenda dying unexpectedly six months after Darlene, and my wonderful mother Pearlie Mae Moore's death just two weeks after Brenda, it all became too much for me. In death, mama taught me the <u>final lesson</u>:

God <u>always</u> provides opportunities where obstacles occur, through the options He gives us if <u>we</u> take them.

Even though focusing on and maintaining our faith is a requirement, a desperate deliverance will only occur by exposing and overcoming the potholes-of-life known as obstacles.

Notes

Chapter Four

The Options for Obstacles

People in general have the same complaint when misfortune occurs: Why are these obstacles in my life? What did I do to deserve this misfortune? When will God remove these obstacles from my path? How can I be expected to be better and not become bitter, when obstacles appear in my way? Grief is an obstacle I never expected to encounter with such magnitude.

The deaths of nearly 60 percent of my closest female relatives proved an obstacle that even I could not fathom. My lesson from all of this: When obstacles occur in our lives, God gives us options to overcome them, and shows us the opportunities He has for us. It honestly took me these past four years to understand and bring it all together; however, my hope is that God's revelation to me will help the reader much sooner in the grieving process.

Obstacles

Deliverance and distress are both caused by the same thing: Obstacles. Merriam-Webster defined an obstacle as "Something that makes it difficult to do something; an object you have to go around or something that blocks your path" (Obstacle, 2015). The bible is replete with examples of obstacles in people's pathway which they could not move; obstacles so difficult that it required a desperate deliverance. People needing a desperate deliverance are often dehumanized and only identified by their condition. The lepers had no names but lepers, and the condition identified the woman with the issue of blood. Even today, people are labeled by their condition, and grieving is just such a condition.

By now it should be apparent that I experienced a tremendous amount of grief from four tragic events that occurred within 11 months. Just as we defined obstacles, grief deserves the same reverence. Grief is defined as "A deep and poignant distress caused by or as if by bereavement; a cause of such suffering" (Grief, 2015). By its very definition, grief is a condition that requires deliverance from distress, most notably the distress caused from death. Randy Peterson (2012) wrote in *When You Lose Someone You Love* that grief begins when it begins and ends when it ends, but stays for as long as necessary.

Through our definitions of grief and obstacles, death can be considered a catastrophic event resulting in the supreme obstacle of grief. Grief as an obstacle, a difficulty to overcome; a blockage in the pathway of life; can paralyze, cripple, and even cause some to succumb to the pressure. Grief will steal your happiness, impact your joy, and make you question your faith, but as with all things, there are options to dealing with grief. During my time of bereavement, God showed me the options available to overcome the obstacle of grief, but more importantly, why only one option made sense.

Options

Because God never leaves or forsakes us, there are always options to our obstacles. An obstacle can be overcome using one of four options: Going through it, over it, under it, or around it. To the naked eye, those options may appear equal, but to the practitioner versed in the trials of the world, there are gradations of success in each option. Although there are four options, only one truly provides the success necessary to overcome the supreme obstacle of grief.

Going Under an Obstacle. Going under anything is almost automatically the least desirable option. To move anything by going underneath, especially an obstacle, is an exercise in ergonomics. Going under an obstacle requires the correct depth, strength, and energy available to move under the obstacle without the obvious occurring: Being crushed under the weight of the obstacle. Going under the obstacle of grief is essentially asking God, *why did this occur?*

The question coupled with the answer is what sometimes provides the weight of obstacles that causes us to be crushed. Going under the obstacle may be rehashing that which is already known: A prolonged illness, precarious lifestyle, a bad relationship, or a victim of circumstance. Whatever the reason, asking

God a question with a known answer is merely creating an unstable obstacle, and inviting the weight to crush us under additional grief. Most people are better suited to go around an obstacle then under it, although traversing the obstacle may bring no greater resolution, relief, or removal of the blockage.

Going Around an Obstacle. Going around an obstacle often seems the best recourse, providing us the means to quickly overcome our hurdle. Sometimes however, going around an obstacle is impossible. People often drive around a pothole in the road however, the supreme obstacle of grief is a sinkhole: Too wide to go around and too deep to climb out from without help. Sometimes attempting to go around an obstacle is tantamount to ignoring the problem. The problem with death is that it is final, no free passes, redoes, or delay of game.

Ignoring a problem does not make the problem disappear but can possibly fester and manifest itself in abhorrent and sometimes ungodly behavior. Going around an obstacle if that is possible, does not remove the obstacle from your pathway, and continues to create a blockage. Whenever you return to the point of the obstacle, it remains, firmly planted, waiting for engagement. This may sometimes lead people to attempt and go through the obstacle, head on and full force.

Going Through an Obstacle. The effort to go through an obstacle is the most easily dismissed, because if you could simply go through it, based on the definition, it would not be an obstacle. Because obstacles come in many shapes and sizes, attempting to meet the obstacle head-on may create an even greater obstacle. Once the supreme obstacle of grief hits you, the realization occurs that the only option available is to go over the obstacle.

Going Over an Obstacle. The attempt to go over an obstacle is where a desperate deliverance begins, and the sovereignty of God is recognized. Going over anything means rising above it, and in the diminished state of grief, how does one rise above anything? But God, is how we rise above not just anything in life, but everything regarding death. Going over obstacles is not something we intuitively think of, but just as God takes us from the valley of the shadow of death (Psalm 23), He provides us the incentive to begin the great climb. Going over an obstacle is the option where Godly measures occur in the form of opportunities. Although the options for obstacles led to opportunities, there may be the necessity to encounter storms along the way.

Notes

....

....

....

....

....

....

....

....

....

....

....

....

....

....

....

....

....

....

....

....

Part II
Don't Waste a Good Storm

As the reader has determined by now, I am fascinated by storms. Storms show God's providence like no other event, because there is nothing that man can do to change the course of events. Meteorologist report, predicts, speculate, and finally, capitulate on what will occur during a storm, but God always knows. God knows that the horrific winds that are sent must sometimes remove things that long outlived their usefulness. God knows that the thunder and lightning is a means to make people sit still. The Lord also knows that the torrential downpours that occur are needed to replenish the land. When all is said and done and the damage is assessed, sometimes people's shattered lives are rebuilt better than before. In essence: Don't waste a good storm.

Little did I know that my storms were just beginning, and God not only asked if He could trust me with trouble but began preparing me for some personal troubles of my own. God grants opportunities to those who would take them, but by failing to recognize my opportunities, a storm began to brew inside of me. Although mama's death should have made me sit down and sit still, I decided to stand in the storm, just like the picture on the cover of this book. The next few months and years tested my faith in ways I never imagined, but also taught me how to recognize and not waste a good storm.

Notes

Chapter Five

Optimizing Opportunities

Realizing that I needed to go over my *supreme obstacle of grief*, I sought Godly measures to work in overcoming my obstacle. The Godly measures given to me were the Opportunity of Decrease, and the Opportunity of Sitting Still, to reflect on losing a child, two sisters, and a parent, all within a period of 11- and one-half months. I needed Godly measures because no matter how hard I tried; I could not raise myself over the obstacles alone. God had to illuminate for me the best method to ascend over my problems. The Lord had to place in my spirit, the means to optimize the opportunities He would provide for me.

The Opportunity of Decrease

The Opportunity of Decrease revealed servanthood at the appropriate time. No matter how long ago your child may have died, it will always seem like yesterday. LaTarsha TeNille Moore had left our lives only 11 months earlier, so the impact of Neal's death certainly remained fresh.

Even though still devastated by Neal's death, the unexpected death of my baby sister Darlene Moore five months later, gave my mother and I a shared experience (between parent and child): Knowing the loss of a child. God allowed and required this shared experience to provide me the Opportunity of Decrease. The

Opportunity of Decrease allows a person to shift (if only temporarily) from an internal to an external focus. This may be done in any manner, through focusing time, talent, and attention away from a more personal obstacle or issue, to focus on someone else's obstacle or issue.

The Opportunity of Decrease when Darlene died allowed me to accomplish two things: Decrease the spotlight from my obstacle of grieving over Neal's murder, to help my mother move over her obstacle of losing her youngest child. The help I provided to my family, but especially my mother, became less pastoral and more experiential. John Dewey (1930) described experiential learning as knowing by doing or having done. I could not have provided the same level of care, compassion, and counsel to mama during Darlene's death, had I not experienced it by losing Neal.

As I previously wrote regarding God's providence, I could not have known how profound that statement would be. As Pastors, we often pray the same prayer before we begin every sermon: *Lord, allow me to decrease so that You may increase, so that Your people may hear Your word.* The concept of decrease to increase makes perfect sense from a scientific perspective because for anything to increase, something must decrease.

Unfortunately, the decrease continued as we lost my middle sister, Brenda Williams, five months after Darlene. As I continued to apply the Opportunity of Decrease, I learned the true meaning of the Opportunity of Increase: I had never ceased grieving or decreasing in regard to Neal, but my attention had merely been diverted with Darlene's passing. Now Brenda's passing brought full force the concept of *decrease* to *increase*, because it validated what I had already known but we sometimes forget:

God always provides our increase,
if we can decrease.

Losing Neal, Darlene, and Brenda within 11 months provided the ultimate decrease for me, and I reacted in the only way I knew how: By serving God and His people with a greater passion and fervor. The only comfort in death is if one knows that a family member knew and served the Lord. I knew that Neal, Darlene, Brenda, and mama all knew God not only because we were all raised in the church, but because we continued to serve the Lord with all our hearts. At this point it is important for me to dispel a myth regarding Christians, who are often referred to as 'Church Folks'.

The myth is: "If they knew the Lord, it makes their passing easier". The knowledge that a loved one knew the Lord does not make their passing any easier, or better. I know this may sound contrary to the clichés of the day, but as Paul wrote, he learned to be content in whatsoever state (Philippians 4:11). Sometimes contentment is all there is after the Opportunity of Decrease because life does not stand still in our grieving state. Further events would cause me to decrease even further, and sometimes a supreme decrease is required just for us to sit still and listen to God's voice.

The Opportunity of Sitting Still

As a Pastor, free time is at a premium. Corporate Chief Executive Officers (CEO) and military Generals execute arduous schedules. Each seeks the maximum return on investment (ROI) for shareholders or in the defense of our nation. A Pastor's schedule, however, is the same but with a different calling. God is the Chairman of the Board and chief shareholder of the corporation I serve, expecting an ROI of saved souls through the salvation of accepting Jesus Christ as Lord and Savior.

I lead, serve, and fight in the Army of the Lord against the greatest enemy mankind has ever known: The devil. The devil seeks to devour who he would and sitting still is not a trait that I am known for, fond of, or use. Based on a person's disposition however, the last Godly measure for taking you over your obstacles may be the Opportunity of Sitting Still.

The Lord had engaged for me the Opportunity of Sitting Still after each tragedy: With the murder of Neal, and after unexpectedly losing Darlene and Brenda. I am a fulltime Pastor of my church and I often tell people:

Serving God is not what I do, but who I am.

My church graciously asked me each time after the tragedies struck beginning with Neal, if I needed to take some time off. I thought I needed to process the events in my own way by serving God and others with an even greater intensity. Truth be told there is an old cliché that the military uses:

It's hard to hit a moving target.

My thought processes were that if I remained active and not sit still too long, I would not have to think about the events. The true Opportunity of Sitting Still came to pass only two weeks after Brenda's unexpected death with the unexpected passing of mama.

As I wrote previously, *Losing Neal meant losing a piece of what I gave her, but losing mama meant losing a piece of what she gave me.* Losing a mother makes a man grow crushingly weary, and just as God rested on the Sabbath day, losing mama caused my spirit to sit still. Losing a mother can immobilize, paralyze, or even cripple a strong man, especially if he fails to heed the need to sit still. If possible, during grief or after a storm, a person should sit still long enough to wonder, speculate, grieve, and reflect.

Most importantly, sitting still long enough allows a person to hear the voice of God, and catch the breath of life. I often tell parishioners to stop listening *to* the noise, and listen *for* the voice of God but sometimes, CEOs only sit still and listen when the Chairman of the Board speaks.

With many of the women, we had known our entire lives gone, my brother, Arthur Moore and I, grew closer to each other, and to God. Our hearts ached however, for our sister Earlene, for as she explained to Arthur and I:

You two can console each other as men, talk for two hours, and make one another feel better. For me, there is no woman to talk with. Both of our sisters and mama are gone. Neither of you can understand the loneliness.

Those comments were sobering and added an even greater need for me to sit still and reflect.

Be Still, Stanley

After 12 months of heartache and pain, God had my full attention now and gave me a message found in Psalm chapter 46, verse 10:

"***Be still, and know that I am God***"

Though God always has my attention, the opportunity of sitting still allowed me to listen to the other messages He shared with me:

Slow down; *Take care of yourself*; *Embrace the family you have*; *Continue My work.*

I often did not execute God's messages in the order given, but my mother's death removed my mask of invincibility. Just as she departed unexpectedly, illnesses began to strike my body that forced me to catch the breath of life.

Being ever so busy and never wanting to slow down, you sometimes never know how much you want or need to catch the breath of life, until you cannot catch your breath. The combination of my mother's death and my own unaddressed illnesses now ensured the Opportunity of Sitting Still that God provided and forced me to reflect on His word. Often, doing nothing is the reward we need, and again, the Lord rested on the Sabbath day.

Sitting still, reflecting, recouping, and reviving is why God gives us the Opportunity of Sitting Still. Through that opportunity, I knew that I wanted to tell my story and share with so many others, how I have made it over the obstacles of life: Through a deep and abiding faith in God and our Lord and Savior Jesus Christ. My days are often long, and my heart still aches for the losses of four of the most important women in my life, but through God's grace and mercy, I am learning to be better, not bitter, about life's events, and how to embrace my own storms.

Notes

....

....

....

....

....

Chapter Six

Better Not Bitter

Embracing my storms became the winter of my discontent. It proved the biggest and the most brutal storm I had ever encountered to that point in my life. Although I am a man of God, I am still only a man, and therefore may lack understanding from time to time. One of those times occurred during this trial. God's will is always perfect but unfortunately, our understanding is not. Losing any of my relatives would cause me great pain, but to lose the dearest of the dear, my mother, became nearly unbearable.

I often tell parishioners to be better, not bitter, but after the previous 12 months, I needed to tell myself that daily. Although anger and/or bitterness may be parts of the grieving process, I do not hold these characteristics in esteem. As a leader of one of God's corporations, I needed a means to avoid the anger and bitterness phase of grief. Learning to embrace my storms provided a turning point in my journey. Embracing my storms, however, did not preclude the storms from moving out of the water, and leaping into my ship.

Stanley's Storms

After my mother's death, I took the opportunity to sit still and listen for the voice. The voice or voices I heard most often were the aches and pains that accompanied my body. If someone produced '**Grief-in-a-Bottle**', no one would buy it because it is too easy to self- manufacture. Keeping your grief inside and not expressing it; is in essence, placing grief in a bottle. My grief-bottle had reached the point of explosion, as my health began to deteriorate before my own eyes, and I felt powerless to do anything about it. By not expressing my grief, I began to sink fast and without a life preserver.

Sinking with Peter

When Peter's faith began to falter while walking on the water, he began to sink. My health and faith took the same turn for the worse as all manner of maladies and ailments arose. It began with a *tiredness* that <u>never ceased</u>, *aches* that continued to <u>increase</u>, and a *restlessness* I could not <u>release</u>. Ulcer this, prostrate that, diabetic whatever, if the doctors named it, I had it, and then the worst event occurred: I became discouraged because I saw defeat. Discouragement is a loss of courage, and I became convinced about the imminence of my death. After all of my test, trials, and now physical illnesses, I had not learned at that point how to embrace my storm.

Don't Waste a Good Storm

God gave me the insight to provide a sermon entitled *Don't Waste a Good Storm*, but the best way to waste it is if you don't embrace it. God needed me to learn how to embrace my own storms to get physically, mentally, and emotionally better, so as to not turn bitter.

Learning to embrace my storms took the better part of the three years that followed but I did it, and so can you.

Embracing Your Storms

There is an old spiritual that has a line which says *Ride out your storm, God will be with you. It may not seem easy but ride out your storm.* Being from the country, a person does not just mount a horse and begin to ride. If the horse senses any anxiety, the horse of course becomes anxious, and transforms into a bronco, a bucking bronco, and riding becomes problematic. A storm is much the same way.

When God allows the storms of life to enter our domain, cease from becoming anxious, and just as you establish rapport with the horse before riding it, we must learn to embrace our storms before riding them out. Embracing our storms has three ships vital for success: Scholarship, Relationship, and Followership. Embracing our storms involves seeking the shelter of God's love, grace, and understanding.

The Scholarship of Storms

The scholarship of a storm consists of knowing the truisms about the storms that God allows in our lives. <u>First</u>, do not look for or wait on miracles, but ask for and recognize mercies. Grieving is grieving irrespective of person, so no miracles will occur to alleviate the process. God does however grant mercies every day to soothe our wounded souls. The life of my grandson Justyn, Neal's son, provided me with mercy. The stalwart support of my wife Connie through these great trials gave me mercy. The care, concern, and compassion of my other children, Kelton (Scooter), Suzanne (Suky), Sabastian (Mel), and Evin granted me mercy. The loving arms of my congregation displayed to me mercy. Awaking everyday became a mercy. I did not need to look far, and neither will you, if you are looking for mercies and not miracles.

Second, when storms occur, learn to thank God more and complain about the situation less. My mercies could have easily become monstrosities, and all gone the other way. I could have lost my grandson, not had the support of my wife, become estranged from my children, and my health could have deteriorated to the point that I could write this book! Once again, finding time to give thanks is an easy task, but a task that only occurs after recognizing your mercies.

Third but most importantly, begin to praise God as soon as the storm begins, until it ends, and before the next one begins. Because sometimes it may require more than one storm to recognize who saved us from the first one, at all costs do not allow your grief to turn into groaning. Praising God will help you to recognize your mercies and alleviate complaining. It may seem counterintuitive to place praising last in scholarship, but when a person is grieving, everything is counterintuitive, and praise is not the first action one embraces. Understanding the scholarship of storms helps cultivate the relationship to embrace the storms.

The Relationship of Storms

Always remember that when storms occur in our lives, Jesus may not *cause* the storms, but he may *allow* the storms. Why Jesus allows the storms is based on the relationship we have with God, the Father, at that time. God permits storms for three reasons:

Perfection, correction, or reflection. When we listen to the noise of the crowd versus listening for the voice of God, sometimes an attention getting method is required.

Storms of Perfection. Not all storms are evidence of wrongdoing, but sometimes reflect the seriousness of the assignment. This is a Storm of Perfection. God has an assignment for all of us, and *if* we follow the path, He has set for us, there *will* be obstacles in the way. God uses storms to teach us how to maneuver *over* our obstacles, because the assignment is so important. Our ability to maneuver the storm places us in our rightful position and perspective to execute God's will. God showed me the importance of my assignment, and just how He needs me to be present and available to help others. Again, listen for God's voice to recognize the importance of the assignment.

Listening for God's voice may sound contrite, and may deter one from asking, *God, what did I do wrong*? The true question is, *God, what am I doing right that you chose me for the assignment*? When you know that you know that you know that you did nothing wrong, thank God for the opportunity to successfully execute the assignment. If you are less certain about your behavior or actions, then you may become the recipient of a storm of correction.

Storms of Correction. When we fail to listen for God's voice, or heed other signs, storms may come our way, again. These are known as Storms of Correction. We all get off track sometimes and need a gentle nudge to return on course. Some people need more than a nudge. Even after weathering a storm, some people return to the behavior or actions that resulted in the storm to begin with!

The storm of correction is likely much harsher than the storm of perfection, because it is designed to remove all doubt about who can save us from the storm. A storm of correction may require family, friends, or finances to dissolve so that we can see God as the only solution. Just as our earthly fathers correct us, God uses storms of correction to save not sear us. There is no need to waste a good storm, by our misinterpretation of its purpose. Let God's grace save you from yourself and move to the next level God has for your life. All storms of correction do not end in physical death, but may be the death of a job, career, relationship, or financial prosperity. Whatever the storm, grieving occurs and only God can deliver us.

Often after experiencing a storm, we too quickly forget what just happened. In some cases, we believe that we are too old or mature to admit wrong-doing, too saved and sanctified to experience a storm, or in the case of storms of perfection, we become Super Saints. Any of those attitudes will result in another storm that causes us to look back, before we can move forward. Storms of correction should always be followed by the Meal of Humility. Some would refer to this as Eating Crow, but whatever foul food is consumed to regulate the spirit, so be it. Reflection should always follow correction, so as to avoid repeating the same mistake and for righting any other wrongs. Righting the other wrongs is where the Storm of Reflection occurs after correction.

Storms of Reflection. Through inspiration, David wrote in Psalm chapter 46, verse 10, "Be still, and know that I *am* God". As people, we are in a constant state of motion, even when there is no place to go. When God speaks to us through a storm, we do one of two things: we respond appropriately or inappropriately. Inappropriate response may bring another storm that requires us to stop in our tracks and look at where God has brought is from. This is known as a Storm of Reflection.

Sometimes in our perfected state, we forget who brought us through the storm, and again we become Super Saints. Because we are successful in our assignment, we begin to proclaim our greatness. Our forgetfulness of where the true glory lies creates the beginning of our next demise. What befalls us in our perfected posture may be ugliness, illness, or even a death - things that stop us immediately.

This is not a storm of correction, but reflection, for God wants you to remember the storm that occurred while climbing the mountain, and how He kept you safe from all hurt, harm, and danger. God wants you back on your knees, looking for mercies, not complaining, but praising the rightness of His power. Reflection is what catches us as we fall from the mountain of perfection, not correction. Correction requires a different type of reflection.

The Storm of Reflection after correction may be the avoidance *by* all those we offended. It may be the hurt *by* all those we mistreated. It may be hearing the honest assessment of the situation *by* those involved. It may be the shame we feel when seeing the situation from a new perspective. The storm of reflection just as the other storms, will never kill us, but cultivates the right attitude in us, which leads to the right spirit. When we sit still and know who God is, we can once again listen for his voice, without all of the noise. As in all things, embracing your storms also involves learning the process of storms beyond scholarship and relationships, and to relearn followership. This helps us to regain the joy and happiness God promised us.

As I learned to better understand my storms, I became better able to embrace and eventually overcome my storms. Remember, do not waste but embrace a good storm. I discovered that although I had learned to embrace my storms, the journey was not over.

Notes

....

....

....

....

....

....

....

....

....

....

....

....

....

....

....

....

....

....

....
....
....
....
....
....
....
....
....
....
....
....
....
....
....
....
....
....
....
....
....
....

Chapter Seven

The Followership in Storms

The scholarship and relationship Jesus had with the disciples began with followership. In Matthew chapter four, verse 19, Jesus told Simon Peter and Andrew to cast their nets aside and follow him, for he would make them fishers of men. They followed Jesus without hesitation. In Matthew chapter 14, verse 27, the disciples were not so affirming towards Jesus, who walked on the water during a storm. Asking for a sign, only Peter answered Jesus' command to Come.

Before, during, and after a storm, Jesus has a message and a command for us: Follow me, go to the other side, or *Come.* After experiencing our storm, there is an expectation of followership, to keep us on the path we desire and, in the will, God has for us. Followership is also about faith, and how we are willing to follow God.

Follow Me

When Simon Peter and Andrew decided to follow Jesus, they gave up everything: Family, friends, and finances without looking back. When God keeps us through a storm, it may be a desperate deliverance situation that requires our immediate obedience. The PSF - Perfection Storm Followership may be responding to an opportunity to good to be true. The

CSF - Correction Storm Followership may be immediately removing us from a bad situation. The RSF - Reflection Storm Followership may be the revelation of an impending storm that God seeks for us to avoid.

Our scholarship and relationship with God through those storms will establish our followership. Our job is to remember who kept us through the storm. This knowledge requires the faith that God is trying to move us to the other side, to keep us progressing. I needed to follow God more to take care of my own health and needs, so that I could better attend to His will.

Go to the Other Side

God never goes backward to move us forward. Our disobedience or complacency is what causes us to move backward. There is no record in the bible of Jesus ever returning the disciples *back* to the shore they left from during a storm. In every instance, Jesus kept moving the disciples forward, even when they were afraid to go. Sometimes Jesus needs us to move to the other side, so that he can work.

In Matthew chapter 14, verses 22-23, Jesus *constrained* the disciples to get into the ship, and go to the other side. Constrained in this sense meant forced. Jesus forced the disciples into the boat, to begin the journey to the other side. Sometimes when God keeps us during a storm, we want to remain in the same place after the storm has passed. Just as Jesus pressed the disciples forward, God sometimes needs to remove us from the situation to either save us from ourselves, avoid a relapse, or because we are in the way. Because God wants us to keep it moving, He sometimes has to move us out of our own way, for our own good.

Jesus dispersed the multitude and then went and prayed. When God disperses our multitude of problems, he needs us to get to the other side, so that family, friends, and fellow Christians can pray for our safe passage and success. Just as after any storm, once the damage is assessed, we move out of the way to allow clean up to begin. We need to allow God to do the same after our storms, and we need to go to the other side. Sometimes as we journey to the other side however, there may be a trial which again test our faith.

Come

In our newfound status after a storm, a trial or new storm may come our way. Instead of relying on God to keep us as He just did, we fall back on what we *think* we know. When the disciples saw Jesus walking on the water, they needed proof they were not seeing a ghost. Sometimes when God is working so well in our lives after a storm, we forget that a new storm is looming on the horizon. When a new storm occurs, even when God assures us that the plan is His, we lose faith and need proof. Jesus met Peter's challenge to walk on the water by exclaiming one word: *Come*.

Jesus did not use fanfare, signs, wonders, or long proclamations to address Peter's challenge, Jesus simply said *Come*. When we pray a specific prayer, and ask Jesus to do something, he may simply tell us to *Come, move forward, leave the position you are in, for me to answer your very specific request*. God expects followership through faith, not fanfare, after he keeps us through a storm. *Come* is the most profound command of the three followership messages, because Jesus used it as a *response* to a request, not as a command. We must continue to listen for God's voice to become good followers after the storm. Listening may help us avoid or reduce new storms.

Just as we are Disciples of Christ, God uses three ships: Scholarship, relationship, and followership, to help us embrace the storms of life. Also not found in the bible, is an occurrence when a person of God drowned. Noah and family survived the great floods, and Jonah survived in the belly of a whale. The Ships of God will always keep us safe and secure, may allow us to become a little wet, and may even test our faith. The Ships of God teach us how to embrace our storms to survive each one. Always remember, Jesus is there to take us through our storms, to cultivate not kill, and to make us better, not bitter. Though our storms may occur longer than we like, storms may remove the obstacles of our incarcerated happiness.

Chapter Eight

Unlocking an Incarcerated Happiness

Today I can laugh and joke through all of my trials and tests, but that did not always occur. Grief incarcerates your happiness in a manner unlike any other trial because whatever brought you the grief may be a permanent situation. I believe it is of the utmost importance to define happiness versus joy, so as to release you from a possibly self-imposed prison.

Happiness is necessary, mentioned profusely in the bible, and an expectation that God has of us. Happiness has to do with your outer affiliations; what is tangible. The presence of people, the excitement of places, and the accumulation of things is what defines our happiness. Conversely, joy comes from realizing the God given strength that resides inside you. With happiness, you can do anything but not everything however, with joy, you can do all things through Christ, which strengthens you (Philippians chapter 4, verse 13).

Although this book is written for everyone, this chapter has major implications and impact for Christian believers. An incarcerated happiness is comprised of a series of struggles, issues, setbacks, and some hurdles that we cannot seem to get over or through, or even go around. The focused faith in Chapter Two began my journey to unlock my incarcerated happiness and became the key to my victories.

Victory is Mine

The capstone of a focused faith is not just recognizing the facts or acknowledging the truths but recalling the truth of God's promises. God promised us victory, but we must be active participants in the process. Embracing your storm with Godly fact not earthly fear is the first step in the process. The fact is, regaining your happiness is warfare and is not for the faint of heart. If the devil can keep your happiness incarcerated through a sinister characteristic known as complacency, the battle is lost. I had to remember that victory is mine but not through mere platitudes, but through hard fought battles and the costs of victory.

The Cost of Victory

Grief can kill, plain and simple, so the battle for happiness is only for those willing to endure or hold on to the end. The battle is hard fought, will yield the territory of your mind if left unattended, is win or lose, and winner take all. Fighting only until you are tired is a sure recipe for death and may cause casualties of those around you. To be victorious in battle is to acknowledge that you are engaged in battle.

The bible is one of the best compendiums of warfare ever written, and provides us the tactics necessary to engage battles. Ephesians chapter six, verses 10-19 outlines for us the clothing of a Soldier, expressing what we need to wear at all times. Adorning the battle gear of a Soldier is no easy task, especially in God's Army, but remember: You are fighting for freedom from grief. The girdle of truth, breastplate of righteousness, and footwear for the preparation of the gospel of peace is only half of the uniform. The shield of faith, helmet of salvation, and sword of the spirit round out the battle attire, but the preparation remains incomplete.

Happiness Unleashed

Dressing like a Soldier does not make one a Soldier or ensure victory. Preparation is one of the keys to victory, and part of preparation is an intimate knowledge of the weaponry of war. The sword of the spirit is the word of God, and the most vital piece of equipment in the armament. The ability to wield the sword with skill and proficiency occurs through hiding the word of God in your heart and speaking the word with conviction. Expectation of victory is one of the final elements necessary to win the battle.

Expecting God to move on our behalf is a necessity because God always keeps his promises. In Romans chapter eight, verse 31, we were promised that "God is for us, In great grace, He stooped to accept us into His family. In immense mercy, He still found us wandering, forgives our foolish ways, and frees us to serve him". Fighting and expectation is how our incarcerated happiness is finally unleashed.

Because fighting and expectation are the means to release our incarcerated happiness, it should be recognized that things will get worse before they get better. Expectations will wane, the fight may require reinforcements, and truth be told, the fight may not be ours at all, but truly the Lords. Christian friends, there are some fights that require more than the tools of war. Just as the children of Israel were ill-equipped to fight the Pharaoh, and God grants us a desperate deliverance from some obstacles, we still may allow the elusive *It* to hold us in bondage.

Family Photos

My Angel

LaTarsha TeNille Moore

'Neal'

Inseparable

L: Brenda Williams (Moore) R: Darlene Moore

You would have thought my loving sisters were twins, they were so inseparable.

Mama and Me

Mama Pearlie Mae Moore with son

Pastor Stanley Moore

The Family

Adults from left to right:
Kelton (Scooter), Suzanne (Suky), and Evin
Children from left to right:
Justyn, Taylor, and Tyler

Sister Sisters

Suky and Neal

Part III

How *It* Impacts Our Lives

The little things in life may have the greatest impact. As I reviewed my notes and ordering of chapters for this book, I noticed that a very small but apparently important word appeared continuously in the last few chapters: *It*. Merriam-Webster (2015) defined *It* in two manners, both of which were pronouns. He, she, him, or her may be the *It* in question, but rarely do we identify people as *It*. The situation defined the next category of *It:* The problem, issue, subject, thing, or event.

Another definition of *It*: the one previously mentioned; an impersonal verb; an anticipatory subject or object; a general condition or state of affairs; a critical situation or culmination, *It* has a wide range of meanings. The *It* in this context is the trouble God has entrusted us with. Paul wrote in I Corinthians chapter 14, verse 33 that "For God is not the author of confusion, but of peace, as in all the churches of the saints" (NKJV). God does not entrust us with what we cannot handle. What God does entrust us with is not always pleasant, and we may not understand it, but God has a purpose for *It*. The necessity to learn more about *It* is vital for us so that God may move us to the next level in His plans for us and learn to trust us with trouble.

Notes Page

Chapter Nine

Don't Let It Linger Any Longer

In a time of immense emotions such as grief, *It* seems to engulf our lives. The *It* I am referring to is the person, place or thing trying to keep us apart from God. During the grieving period, *It* can be defined as the critical situation or culmination of events. *It* may be an estranged loved one, the newfound wealth that a situation brought, or the financial heartache. The *It* during grieving may not be unique to grieving but surfaced prominently during that time. Whether grieving, groaning, or even growing, any *It* that seeks to keep you apart from God must be dealt with before *It* buries your blessing. The best means to address *It* is by identifying it, not tolerating it, and ultimately destroying it, before *It* destroys you.

Identify *It*

As previously written, *It* may come in many forms, as a person, place, or thing. The key to identifying *It* is the impact *It* has on your relationship with God. Bereavement may cause our minds to be in a state of disequilibrium because of the transition that is occurring (Mikulincer & Florian, 1995), between continuing to live life while accepting the death of a loved one. Bereavement may be the *It* that pushes us away from God. As a man of God, I could not allow this and because of His tender mercies, God kept me close by Him.

Because change is one of the greatest difficulties for man, transitions may also create a huge *It* that causes us to turn from God. Dating, graduating, moving, or celebrating our newfound success may cause us to forget about God. The *It* in your life can be circumstances that stop you from attending church, fellowshipping with other Christians, to stop reading the bible, and to ultimately, stop praying. This may involve family, friends, coworkers, other Christians, a situation, or a mindset. Whatever the *It* that is impeding your life, once identified, you must no longer tolerate it.

Don't Tolerate *It*

Tolerate is a much-misused word in our society. Tolerate is between liking and disliking because to tolerate means to *allow* what you do not *like*. We often do not tolerate things we do not like: Food, clothing, television shows, people, etc. We release or avoid all those things we do not like, except *It*. We tolerate *It* because *It* may be something we do not like but is more than likely something that does not like us: Sin. Just as there are many sins, there are many *It*'s, both of which may keep us from moving forward.

What is your *It*, and is *It* a sin? Anger, vengeance, gluttony, slothfulness, impatience, mean-spiritedness, and unforgiveness are just a few of the *It*'s that we have, we tolerate, but are also sins. Most importantly, each of those *It's* you can do alone: Gain weight, be lazy, be impatient with everything and everyone. Mean-spiritedness, anger, vengeance, and unforgiveness can be solitary endeavors for two simple reasons I call the 50/50 Fiasco. The 50/50 Fiasco consist of 50 percent of those we have ill feelings against are unaware, and the other 50 percent don't care.

Do not tolerate *It*, because *It* will only cause you loneliness, misery, and lead you to depression and possibly other things. Discover the *It* in your life that is making you so desperately miserable, and ask God to give you the strength to no longer tolerate *It*, to remove *It*, and to eliminate *It*. If the *It* you retain is the self-pity or bitter spirit that sometimes accompanies grief, then *It* may need to be destroyed.

Destroy *It*

As a minister for 25 years, people always ask me *What is the one thing (sin) that God cannot forgive?* That question is tragic for two reasons. First, it accentuates the negative by looking for what manner of mischief can be conducted but remain safe under God's arc. The problem with that line of thinking is that although God may forgive the sin or thing, there will still be consequences. God forgives the bank robber if he/she asks, but they still go to jail if/when caught. God delivers and forgives the drug addict or alcoholic if they ask, but much of the physical damage may already be done or seen years later. It is better to struggle with doing right, than to suffer for doing wrong.

The second reason is that there is not one unpardonable sin, but two. Most Christians understand the unpardonable sin of blasphemy or proclaiming there is no God. The other, more prevalent and most pervasive sin that Christians face: Unforgiveness. God cannot work with the unforgiving spirit, because God is a God of choice, and the unforgiving spirit has chosen a hardened heart. God does not force us to love, hate, or forgive however, because all three are choices, God has also chosen not to attempt to work through unforgiveness. Unforgiveness in man is tantamount to disbelief in God's healing power. In other words, unforgiveness is a lack of faith in God. During periods of grief, some people want to place blame. Some people even go as far as blaming God. That spirit must be destroyed quickly and thoroughly.

I could have chosen many *It*'s to address destroying, but the *It* of unforgiveness destroys more lives than any other. Because the rationale of unforgiveness is so subjective, normally only the person harboring *It* truly knows why the condition exists. If there is anyone in your life that you have not forgiven for any reason, the solution occurs in two parts. First, pray to forgive them through God's healing power. This may not be immediate, and praying more than once is authorized, but prayer is required and only God can heal you.

Second, ask God for forgiveness for yourself, for harboring the feelings of unforgiveness and literally hatred for so long. Both may take more than one prayer requests, but God will answer both prayers, heal you, and allow you to move on with your life. Blaming God for the inevitable serves no purpose. We must work through our grief, but do not blame God, or anyone else for the situation of death.

Now that *It* has been identified, no longer tolerated, and even possibly destroyed, now what? Because God is sovereign, and can use all things how He sees fit, you are not done with *It*. As written in the introduction to Part III, *It* is very prolific and can occur in many areas of our lives, and will. It is just a matter of identifying how *It* is used, and although joy comes in the morning, so do trials, tribulations, and tumultuous situations. In those instances, *It*'s just part of the process.

Notes

....

....

....

....

....

....

....

....

....

....

....

....

....

....

....

....

....

....

....

....

....

....

....

....

....

....

....

....

....

....

Chapter Ten

It's Just Part of the Process

At a certain juncture in my journey, God still asked me if He could trust me with trouble. At the time, I honestly I did not know the answer, because I had never experienced this type of trouble. As a pastor, you become accustomed to dealing with other people's troubles: Life, death, and every problem in between. You provide the best God-given advice possible: Words of encouragement, solace, and rejuvenation, with reassurances that the storm is not forever, and that it will make you better, not bitter. Just as the cliché: Physician, heal thyself, the same can be said for pastors: Pastor, save thyself. Unfortunately, that cliché for pastors is impossible, so prayer and supplication must suffice.

Pray that I might, day and night, with deep and abiding faith, the pain of my losses would not subside. Even with the abundance of all God's blessings, I thought that my pain remained just part of the grieving process. I soon learned what most people do not know: The pain associated with grieving is not just part of *a* process, but part of *the* process. Birth, growth, graduation, work, marriage, child rearing, retirement, old age, and death, it's all just part of the process.

Life is a process, and any effort to circumvent that process results in negative consequences. People progress in life along a standardized path, but as written previously, that path is fraught with obstacles. When an obstacle is encountered, God uses four tools to help us over the obstacle: Obedience, intervention, restoration, and guidance.

Obedience

Obedience is another one of the most difficult tasks for mankind, and the difficultly seems even greater for Christian's. It is written in I Samuel chapter 15, verse two that obeying is better than sacrifice. Obeying is not just an acknowledgement of hearing God's voice, but a willingness to submit to God's will. In Psalm 23, David wrote that the Lord was his shepherd that he shall not want. Want, in that sense meant all of David's needs were fulfilled. David next wrote that He (God) made him lay down.

Making David lay down is where the obedience began. God cannot work to begin our healing, until He has our full attention. Obedience signifies we are listening and obeying God. God knows just what we need in our time of grieving, and when we need it most. If we obey, we begin to see and feel the signs of healing. The signs may not seem significant, or the feelings profound, but processes take time. That is why God's intervention is the next part of the process, and where the healing truly begins.

Intervention

Intervention is at the crux of the Christian life. Jesus' sacrifice on the cross served as an intervention for us with the Father. Jesus and the Holy Spirit continue to intervene for us daily, although we do not recognize it, or acknowledge it when we do. God intervenes for us in good times as well as bad, but the bad times are what we remember most.

The Lord required David to lie down in green pastures to provide him comfort. The Lord then led David near the still waters, which provided him calmness. The combination of the green pastures and still waters denoted safety and security from the calamity of the events that occurred. This also describes the opportunity of sitting still, as mentioned earlier. Do not let anyone tell you that there is peace in grieving, because there is none. The mind is swirling with every illogical thought imaginable as to why the situation cannot be denied. Without the ability to lie down in that green pasture, next to the still waters, a grieving person may not ever sleep, eat, or function normally again.

We must recognize God's tool of intervention for just what it is: The means to save us from ourselves. No amount of praying will ever change the events of the past but can shape the desires for the future. Let God's healing power work on you until God is ready to promote you to the next level: Restoration.

Restoration

When God restores our soul, which only He can do, it provides Him another opportunity to show His grace and mercy. Because grieving moves our lives out of order, God wants to bring us back into order. Shelia Walsh (2011) wrote that "*The storms of life are not discriminating. We all experience them no matter our age or status*" (p. 7). Just as grieving is a slow process, so is restoration. God must soothe our wounded spirit, ease our cluttered mind, and allow us time to understand that the process is not a punishment. We soon realize that although God is restoring our soul, He is not necessarily restoring us to our former position. Grieving serves a purpose that only God can make us understand, as He continues to lead us and guide us in the direction, He wants us to go.

Guidance

David also wrote in Psalm 23 that *"He leads me in the path of righteousness"*. Righteousness is defined as virtue, morality, uprightness, and justice. Honesty and blamelessness are also two definitions of righteousness, and two terms of great impact when grieving. God must show us what we may not want to see: Some signs, symptoms, or signatures surrounding previous events. Some truths that we saw but could not see clearly at the time. The revelations of the knowns and unknowns in other people's lives, none of which we were privy too. This is where the honesty is revealed, however painful, but also the blamelessness.

Often in grieving, we lay blame at the feet of those least likely to have caused the situation: God and ourselves. There is never a need to blame God for anything negative, because even if it were true, we are not in a position to do anything about it. Blaming God is always a losing proposition, because the main one hurt in that situation is us. God does not change, nor is He called to serve us, but does correct and protect us. Self-blame is also a worthless endeavor, because we have but limited power on this earth, and only limited influence over others.

God leads us in the path of righteousness to help guide us through the valley of the shadow of death called blame and grieving. God leads us and feeds us in our great moments of despair. Our job is to follow where He leads, and swallow what He feeds. God is leading us to the next level He requires us at in our walk with Him, and the journey of our lives. God is feeding us the pills of promotion: Courage, honesty, blamelessness, discernment, and revelation.

Promotion, not Punishment

Through all our grief and despair, life goes on. People continue to pick and pluck at us, and some even find reasons to fear and hate us. Those people seek to keep us in the valley of despair, bitter and broken. Therefore, God prepares the table for us with our enemies, so the enemies can see the anointing directly from God. At that table, God also serves us the cup of life for all to see.

As our cup fills and overflows, there are two purposes: Correction and perfection. As we grieve, in our minds the world contracts and everything seems smaller. As we begin to emerge from the valley however, we will start to receive unexpected and unrequested blessings. God then allows the cup to run over to correct our thinking, and to show that we not only have a cup, but a mug that has an abundance of blessings! The perfection is to show our enemies that although we may look down, that we are not out and have received a promotion from the valley.

The promotions from the valley are in the forms of mental, physical, and emotional prosperities. Because material matters are unimportant to the griever, the ability to smile, laugh, and stop crying are promotions. A doctor's good report on our health is a promotion. The ability to sleep well at night is a promotion. Whatever grief took from us, God restores and exceeds, sometimes tenfold. For those who allow it, grieving can evolve into a promotion and not a punishment, but it's all just part of the process. Another part of the process is the assurance that goodness and mercy will follow us all the days of our lives. This can only occur if we do not grant the grief a supreme greatness in our lives, and by understanding that things may not be as bad as they seem.

Chapter Eleven

It's Not as Bad as It Seems

As I pondered how to continue moving forward, many things came to mind as it often will in a grieving state. Just give up, give out, or give in, as Job's friends and wife told him, encouraged, I am certain, by the devil. The story of Job is the measure of a man who lost everything, not because of anything he did wrong, but because of his status as an upright man of God. Although God allowed Satan to torment Job, God still needed to know from Job: *Can I trust You, Job, with Trouble*? God wanted Job to know that no matter how bad it got, and it got downright dismal for Job, it's not as bad as it seems, when we admit, affirm, and anticipate God's saving grace.

Admit Conflict

Too often in our society we receive mixed messages. One message says that *It's OK to grieve, show your emotions, let it all out.* The more popular cliché is that *Women grieve, but men move on.* Taking both philosophies at face value, how can you accomplish both? As a man, I will tell you that the cliché is often how most men deal with grief because that is how men are taught to act: Solemn, solitary, and sullen. Men must put on a strong facade and move forward for our families, our jobs, and our friends. We ignore how we feel and just keep it moving.

Dear readers, here is another myth I must dispel in the name of Jesus. Nowhere in the bible does it say that a man cannot, does not, or should not grieve the loss of loved ones, but we somehow follow that flawed philosophy. Job finally came to grips with his situation, after he admitted a situation existed. Job did not actually lament or express how he felt about his situation until Chapter Three of the book of Job.

We must admit that there is a conflict or trouble, and in this case, that conflict or trouble is grieving. Grieving is a natural and normal part of the human condition. When Job stopped defending his position, but recognized *It*, he gained solace from his conflict. When we admit conflict without complaining, God will see us through *It*, like He did for Job.

Affirm Confidence

Job never complained to his three friends or to his wife about the situation. He never cursed God about his situation or believed that God had abandoned him. Job knew that complaining most often leads to evil intentions, and that is why God does not condone it. After Job expressed his grief and God spoke to him, he knew beyond a shadow of a doubt that God remained in his corner.

Once Job reaffirmed in his heart that God remained in his corner, his attitude changed. After we admit our conflict, whether it is grief, loneness, or despair, and cry out for God's healing hand, we begin to see the light of day again. Job had a prayer, and so do we all: To be lifted from our conflict and reestablished anew. As we begin to see God work, our confidence in life also begins to resume. Our confidence in life is affirmation of our trust in God. Praying to God is only part of the prayer process but believing in our own prayer is also the other important aspect. We have not because we ask not, but also because we believe not. With his confidence restored, Job began to celebrate life again.

Anticipate Celebration

Hebrews chapter 11, verse one tells us that "*Now faith is the substance of things hoped for, the evidence of things not seen*". Many people become confused on this passage of scripture, believing the emphasis is on hope. We all hope in anticipation of change, but faith is what sustains our hope. Admitting conflict and affirming confidence are not only signs of trust, but of faith. Admitting conflict shows that we have enough faith in God to admit our vulnerabilities. Affirming confidence shows how much we trust God but requires faith. Job began to praise God and celebrate *before* being 'completely out of the woods,' as we say in the country. Job's *substance of things hoped for* initiated his communication with God, and the understanding he received. Job's *evidence of things not seen* began with the miraculous healings that began to occur all over his body. Faith is what sustained Job through his conflict.

The story of Job provided a great example of what we must do in our valley moments, or Job-like situations: Keep our heads up, know that the Lord is our shield and our salvation, and begin to celebrate before we see the victory. Although this may seem contrary to the human mind, that may be because the human mind cannot deliver us from our plight. Only the spiritual mind can do that. God showed Job that although he had lost everything, *It* was not as bad as *It* seemed. The belief or lies that Job was being punished for his sins were dispelled, because Job had committed no sins.

Although we live in the physical world, we communicate with God, and he solves our problems through a spiritual means. That is why admitting conflict, affirming confidence, and anticipating celebration is such an important remedy in realizing that the storm is not as bad as *It* seems. Just as Job confronted his detractors in the form of his friends and family, we must do the same when they commit what I call Spiritual Malpractice.

Spiritual Malpractice is when we misdiagnose other people's problems. Job's three friends incorrectly misdiagnosed that Job merely needed to repent of his sins, and God would restore him. Job however, had not committed a sin. Job's wife also misdiagnosed that cursing God would cure all of Job's problems, and Job quickly corrected her, because he knew his redeemer lived. We must pray and keep a spirit of praise to find peace in times of profound pressure. After we realize that *It* is not as bad as *It* seems, we then must learn to live with *It*.

Chapter Twelve

Learn How to Live with It

Finally, after learning how to embrace your storms, and learning the process, the final phase of better-not-bitter is learning how to live with it. Learning to live with it or how to live with it, is a cliché as old as time. Some people will tell you to *Man or Woman up*, or *You can take it*, or *don't give up*. As the other cliché goes, *sounds good, briefs well*, unless you are *in* the predicament. In that case, you need to learn how to live with *It*.

Learning to live with *It,* whatever *It entails* is impossible because there are some things beyond our comprehension. Learning *how* to live with *It* is necessary, not complex, earth shattering, or beyond the limits of human endurance. Learning *how* to live with *It* occurs after, and only after, we place it in God's hands. Learning how to live with *It* is God's method to teach us how to be balanced between blessings and burdens. Perfected, precise, and proven, carefully orchestrated to strategic seasons, times, and purposes, God's prescription on how to live with *It* lies in His word, our wounds, our witness, and His wonder.

God's Word

Often acknowledged as one of the most comprehensive and referenced books in the world, the bible is God's living, breathing word. If one were to sit and ponder the many laws, customs, courtesies, and rituals man follows, they could almost all be traced back to the bible in one form or another. God's word is not simple, but it is soothing, and teaches us how to act, how to respond, and how to be in times of trouble. A revelation through writing this book is to begin a grieving ministry or support group. That group would teach people what the bible says about grieving, what it means, and how to process the experience. God's word is a salve to our wounds.

Our Wound

People often attribute wounds only to military service members, police officers, and victims or participants in violent crimes, but we all carry wounds. Falling from a bicycle as a child created a wound. Exiting a bad relationship created a wound. Sufferers of Post-Traumatic Stress Disorder or PTSD, carry an open wound. These examples all have two things in common: All addressed the causes of wounds, and all wounds serve as reminders of something best forgotten.

Our wounds are the reminders of when we were bruised, battered, or broken, but God gave us mercy, and tended to our wounded mind, body, or spirit. Wounds are a means of humbling an unrepentant spirit.

Wounds are a method to make us sit still. Wounds are a manner to create our witness.

Our Witness

The first time I truly laughed after all my heartache, pain, and suffering, I knew that I would be a better witness for God. I knew God's word, my wounds were healing, and through all his grace and mercies, I found the strength to witness in a manner that I had never witnessed before. God healed my wounds and not only kept my soul but saved my earthly life. God's word and our wounds create our witness for Him. Only after we reach this stage, can we appreciate and share God's wonder.

God's Wonder

The beauty of God's Wonder is that it is something only He can do. Family, friends, and finances will not cure the problem, just asks Paul. Paul had an affliction of a thorn in his side that he requested three times for God to remove. The pain from the thorn in his side did not cause Paul's problem, but rather the pride in his attitude. Paul's affliction served the same purpose that each of our afflictions serve: To give us humility in our condition. Once you recognize your condition, whether you feel too short or too tall, believe you read too slowly, or you act too fast, put it in God's hand and learn how to live with it.

Prior to Paul, Jesus prayed three times for a different outcome, but once the Father gave the answer,

Jesus learned *how* to live with the knowledge of his impending death. I praise God every day that Jesus did not rebuke but replied in an affirmative! I will proclaim Hallelujah for us all because without him, this book would not be written! In Chapter Nine, *Don't Let It Linger Any Longer*, we discussed the word tolerate. Tolerate is only found six times in the bible, all in the New Testament, and within three of the four gospels – Matthew, Mark, and Luke (not John), regarding Sodom and Gomorrah from the Old Testament. I mention this because living is not about tolerating but celebrating. Whatever our affliction, once we know it and accept it, not only can we learn *how* to live with it, but God will bless us despite it!

Paul's affliction did not stop him from a successful ministry, and neither should yours. Whatever affliction you have, learn how to live with *It*, make the most of *It*, and get around *It*. The sooner you learn how to live with *It*, the less stress your life will experience, and then you can be like Mike (Michael Jordan) and not *Just Do It* but Do It Now!

Part IV
Through It All

Although the journey may seem endless, it does end at some time when God see's you through it. God see's us through all things we desire to be seen through. Let me write that again: *God see's us through all things we desire to be seen through.* Sometimes we serve as our own obstacle.

Through it all is the epilogue to my journey, and hopefully through yours. It is the epilogue to my journey because through it all, I desired to be healed. Hanging on to what we cannot change may be why our grief never subsides. If we never desire to *get* through it, then we will never *go* through it: The complete grieving process. Our happiness then remains incarcerated. The saying of *Let go and let God* is not a cliché, but a reality of how we go through it all. Through it all is how I got better without being bitter. Through it all is what released my happiness. Through it all is how I let go, and let God, and so can you.

Notes

....

....

....

....

....

....

....

....

....

....

....

....

....

....

....

....

....

....

....

....

My Epilogue: *I'm Still Here*

Do It Right Now!

An amazing life often glossed over in biblical teaching is Noah. Yes, the story of Noah's Ark is often recounted many times, in many forums, and every time there is a major flood in the world. Noah is an amazing *Can God Trust You with Trouble?* story that is lost on many. Charged by God with many tasks, Noah set about each one diligently and with quickness for completion. Noah gave three messages, the first message being *Repent, for the end is near*. Though well respected and well regarded, Noah's neighbors essentially ignored his words but observed his deeds. Noah's second message provided even greater perplexity at the time when he announced: *It's gonna rain!* Noah's neighbors were perplexed by his diligent construction of something called an *ark*, and his prediction of something called *rain*.

Because it had never rained, Noah's messages and behavior seemed foreign. I imagine what began as ignoring or avoiding by Noah's neighbors, quickly turned to ridicule as Noah hammered away endlessly building the ark. Sometimes when God tells us *It's gonna rain*, we ignore Him or avoid the call, because of our narrow-mindedness. Why Noah listened to God and endured the journey is recorded as an act of faith, by a man of faith. With that in mind, imagine that only seven people heard Noah's <u>third</u> message: *I'm Still Here*.

A gospel song by the acclaimed Williams Brothers, *I'm Still Here* recounts how through the trials of life God kept them through another day's journey to carry on. How many of us can say the same? This is my testimony as well, *I'm Still Here*, determined to serve the Lord, do His will, and to **Do It Now**, just like Noah. You never know when the next flood is coming.

Helpless is not Hopeless

Still here and fighting the good fight, grieving may sometimes leave us with a feeling of helplessness. This should be expected because in all actuality, there is nothing we can do to reverse the final verdict, but I am here to proclaim that helpless is not hopeless. Sometimes the helpless feeling is just what we need to move closer to God, lean on Him, and rely totally on Him to renew our strength. Hopelessness is a tool of the devil to deceive and convince us that God has turned His back on us, walked away from us, and forsaken us. This is totally false!

Never in the history of man or womankind has God turned his back on us, walked away from us, or forsaken us. When we cannot seem to find God, it is because <u>*we*</u> moved, He did not. God has never moved from his throne of grace and mercy, but we continually, repeatedly, and sometimes purposely move out of His will, hence our lost and helpless feeling. Let me share why helpless is not hopeless: Because God blesses who He will.

In all His sovereignty, God decides who He will bless, when He will bless them, and why He will bless them. Any influence we might have comes exclusively from being in God's will. Take for example, the blind man who Jesus healed. The most interesting fact about the healing: The blind man never asked to be healed. Jesus just happened by and restored the blind man's sight as an opportunity to demonstrate his power. Helpless is not hopeless when you believe God is on your side. Oftentimes, even when we see God's healing power, miracles, and blessings, we do not believe it. That is why eyesight is so unreliable when seeking God's blessings.

Use Insight not Eyesight

Although the blind cannot see, it is said that the other senses have a heighten awareness. *I'm Still Here* not because of what I can and have seen, but what I can and have *perceived.* To overcome the feeling of helplessness, reliance on the natural senses must give way to the spiritual senses. Eyesight must be replaced with insight, also known as discernment. Simply expressing that *This Too Shall Pass* will not cause it to pass, unless we can see past the circumstances. In addition to the blind man not asking to be healed, there is no record that the blind man ever complained about being blind. We may never know the blind man's discernment, but he knew that a blessing had occurred for him.

I knew from the outset that each of the circumstances that occurred in my Job-like experience were permanent, but with a temporary heartache that felt permanent. Even with that knowledge, I still needed to discern that God would bless me during and after enduring my Job-like journey. Job's eyesight is not what kept him focused, but his insight that he had done nothing wrong, God would keep him covered, and that the future held a better-not-bitter circumstance, is what gave him strength.

After Job cried for what he had lost, he then cried for what he had won: Renewed favor in God's eyes and promise of blessings tenfold! Until we garner the insight to stop using eyesight, our lives will continue to regress from only seeing through hindsight, which hinders our foresight. Through it all, we are *Still Here*, and God continues to call our names to play our positions on His roster. No matter the sacrifice, we must gather strength to do what God commands, right now.

Do It Right Now!

Although cars are designed to move forward, some people become experts at looking through the rearview mirror. Driving in reverse is not a significant measure on any drivers test however, failure to move forward properly and when told to do so, and you will fail the test! Much is the same with God, so sometimes when you are given guidance, Do It Right Now! Because God is predictive and man is fickle, *Do It Right Now* is a message of opportunity, progress, and deliverance. *Do It Right Now* may be the difference between a meaningful and significant advancement and a stagnant and regressive state.

Sometimes our need to understand and control eliminates our opportunity and blessing, because we wait when God tells us to move. We are told exactly what to do, how to do it, when to do it, why to do it, and are made privy to the results, but fail to pursue God's blessings. Sometimes, it is better to thank God for what we do not see and pursue with fervor what He does show us. *I'm Still Here* because I have learned that whatever God calls me to do, I need to ***Do It Right Now***.

Because I execute quickly whatever God tells me to do, my veil of darkness and despair has been lifted. God knew that writing this book provided a means to my healing, but also made me realize that although I am still here, the journey is not over. I still require a plan for what to do until this leg of the journey ends.

Notes

Our Epilogue: *What to Do in the Meantime*

Survival in a Foreign Land

Although this is the epilogue, this is not the end of the story for you or for me. As I continue to travel in a foreign land, God continues to guide me. I have my good days, and my not so good days, but God sees me through them all. The foreign land I travel in is called grief. There is only one way in - through tragedy, and one way out - through God. The tragedy is the trouble, and the trust is in God.

The Israelites were first taken into captivity in 597 BC but did not become an independent nation again until 1948. That period of 70 years is what God needed, two generations, to cleanse the Israelites of wrong minds and wrong thinking that created wrong hearts toward Him. God kept the Israelites in bondage until completion of the mission. Seventy is the number of completions, and although God would not have us grieve 70 years, God does want us to stay with the mission until completed.

Jeremiah chapter 29, verses 4-14 disclosed to the Israelites, who, what, when, where, why, how, and how long their captivity to the Babylonians would take place. Seventy years is a long time in captivity, or to even feel as if you are in captivity. The Israelites asked the same question then that we do today:

What can I do in the meantime?

As mentioned earlier, God told the Israelites every facet of their captivity, including what to do in the meantime. God's plan of productivity, prayer, praise, and promotion worked well for the Israelites, and can also work just as well for us.

Productivity

God told the Israelites to find land, find spouses, begin families, and contribute to the foreign land. In essence, the first command the Israelites were given: **Be productive**. God had no intentions of allowing the Israelites to be released from captivity until the mission to change their hearts occurred. During times of trouble, grief may become our captor, but we can become our own jailer. Even prisoners are allowed a certain number of freedoms and activities. Too often we refuse to move forward in life during a period of grief, regardless of the grace and mercy God has shown us, thereby becoming our own jailers.

God wants only what is best for us during the good and bad times. God does not allow the world to stop when trouble comes but requires us to keep looking through the windshield versus the rearview mirror. When captive in the foreign land of grief, keep pressing forward, doing God's will, and the routine things of everyday life. Do not become passive, but be productive in every facet of your life, especially your prayer life.

Prayer

Productivity will not be automatic in times of trouble or captivity, and we will all need God's help. God instructed the Israelites to pray for their Babylonian captors and praying for our oppressors is what God instructs in all situations. During grief, we have two oppressors or captors: The grief of the heart and of our faith. I Thessalonians chapter five, verse 17 instructs us to *Pray without ceasing* because we are our most vulnerable when we feel that our heart is broken and can never be mended.

Our faith then comes into question, and we may listen to all kinds of false prophets to help us through the pain. Let me be clear: No medicine, drug, or alcoholic beverage will change the situation in a positive manner. No amount of evangelism, laying of hands, or outside prayer will help, unless we pray for our captors as God instructed. Pray for peace, tranquility, productivity, and promotion. Promotion during captivity may sound backwards, but that is not only why we pray to God, but why we praise Him for everything He does in our lives.

Praise

I have written this several times throughout this story: Praise God and stop complaining. Complaining simply blocks our blessings and the ability to prepare for promotion. Complaining is what kept the children of Israel wandering in the desert for 40 years. Complaining is why Job turned his back on his friends. Complaining is how Jonah ended up in the belly of a whale.

Once the complaining stopped, promotion occurred in each situation. Joshua led the children to tumble the walls of Jericho, Job passed the test and received a tenfold blessing, and Jonah continued to and completed the assignment at Nineveh. Because life does not stop while in captivity so praise in the meantime until the promotion arrives.

Promotion

Captivity does not always mean incarceration, as captivity occurs in many forms: Custody, detainment, imprisonment, or internment. The Babylonians did not intern or imprison the cream of the Israeli crop, nor merely hold them in custody. The only avenue left is detainment, which means to delay, keep, hinder, or hold back. Captivity holds us back from what we were doing but prepares us for the future God has for us. We receive the promotion when we can answer the question for ourselves:

Can God trust **me** *with trouble?*

The answer is a simple yet elusive one. God can only trust us *with* trouble, when we can trust Him when there is *no* trouble. always Trusting in God but especially in prosperity is the affirmation that God can trust us with trouble.

As my journey continues, I am blessed to report that not only is my faith in God renewed, but also, His faith in me, His humble servant. I work daily to be productive and a blessing to others. I praise when my eyes open each morning. I pray for strength, joy, and happiness daily for me and for others. And the promotion? God can trust me with trouble today, tomorrow, and forever, and this book is my promotion. I pray that this book has been of the benefit, comfort, and illumination for you to read it, as it was for me to write it.

Praise His holy name!

Author's Abbreviated Biographies

Rev. Stanley Moore

Pastor Stanley Moore served the Lord all his life, and as a minister of the gospel for over 30 years. He served as the Pastor for Progressive Baptist Church in Davenport, IA, from 2005 – March 2022. During his tenure, Pastor Moore has licensed over 25 ministers of the gospel and established the Hope Center at the Lincoln Academy. Previously, Pastor Moore has served as a deacon, Sunday School Superintendent, associate minister, Pastor, and over 30 years as a certified industrial, electrical, and mechanical engineer. Pastor Moore went to be with the Lord in March 2022.

Burl W. Randolph, Jr.

Burl W. Randolph, Jr. is a retired Army Military Intelligence Colonel with nearly 32 years of service, and three combat tours in Iraq. Randolph last served as the Deputy Chief of Staff for Intelligence and Security, Rock Island Arsenal, IL, and is currently a third-year doctoral student with the University of Phoenix. He currently serves as nonprofit Boards of Directors and is the Founder, President, Chief Consultant for MyWingman, LLC, a Business Leadership and Management Consulting company he formed in Davenport, IA. Colonel Burl is also Dr. Burl, with a Doctor of Management in Organizational Leadership.

References

Dewey, J. (1937/1997). *Experience and education*. New York, NY: Kappa Delta Pi/Touchstone. New York, NY: Simon and Schuster

Feldman, R. (2003). *Epistemology*. Upper Saddle River, NJ: Prentice Hall.

Grief. (2015). In *Merriam-Webster*. Retrieved from http://www.merriam-webster.com/dictionary/grief

Mikulincer, M., & Florian, V. (1995). Stress, coping, and fear of personal death: the case of middle-aged men facing early job retirement. *Death Studies*, *19*(5), 413-431. doi: 10.1080.07481189508253391

Obstacle. (2015). In *Merriam-Webster*. Retrieved from http://www.merriam-webster.com/dictionary/obstacle

Peterson, R. (2012). *When you lose someone you love*. Lincolnwood, IL: Publications International Ltd.

Swindoll, C. R. (2012). Nothing helps like hope. An excerpt from Charles R. Swindoll's *Wisdom for the Way: Wise Words for Busy People*. Nashville, TN: J. Countryman, a division of Thomas Nelson, Inc, 2001. Retrieved from http://daily.insight.org/site/News2?page=NewsArticle&id=20163

Walsh, S. (2011). *God's shelter for your storm*. Nashville, TN: Thomas Nelson

Made in the USA
Las Vegas, NV
19 May 2022